PANDAS

Edited by Gretchen Bratvold
Printed in Hong Kong

98   99   00   01   02   5   4   3   2   1

Library of Congress Cataloging-in-Publication Data
Angel, Heather.
Pandas / Heather Angel.
p.   cm. — (World life library)
Includes bibliographical references (p. 71) and index.
ISBN 0-89658-364-3
1. Giant panda. 2. Red panda. I. Title. II. Series.
QL737.C214A54   1998
599.789—dc21   97-42001
                                                         CIP

Distributed in Canada by Raincoast Books, 8680 Cambie Street, Vancouver, B.C. V6P 6M9

Published by Voyageur Press, Inc.
123 North Second Street, P.O. Box 338, Stillwater, MN 55082 U.S.A.
612-430-2210, fax 612-430-2211

On page one: A giant panda in winter in the Wolong Reserve in Sichuan.
On page four: An eighteen-month-old panda rests in the fork of a tree during winter.

PANDAS

Heather Angel

Voyageur Press

Contents

Acknowledgements

Many people helped me to produce this book. Most especially, Director Zhang Hemin of the Wolong Centre for the Conservation and Research of the Giant Panda and his staff, and Keren Su for photography of pandas in natural enclosures. Also in China, Huang Yan, Luo Kai Yue, and Wu Ling assisted by guiding and interpreting during my winter trip. In Great Britain, the WWF-UK, the Zoological Society of London, and Peter Bircher of Marwell Zoo were most helpful providing information. I am especially grateful to Stuart Chapman of the WWF-UK who read and commented on the entire manuscript, and I am greatly indebted to Dr. Robin Pellew, director of the WWF-UK, for writing the foreword. Valerie West, Lindsay Bamford, and Ralph Bower all assisted with the mammoth task of editing the pictures amassed from three trips and deciphering my handwritten copy into a readable text. Not least, grateful thanks to my husband, Martin Angel, for tolerating my frequent departures to China and invaluable help with editing the text.

Note: In the United States and Canada, the WWF is known as the World Wildlife Fund; elsewhere it is known as the World Wide Fund for Nature. To avoid confusion, throughout this book the name of this organization has been abbreviated to simply WWF.

A panda feeds on its favorite food, bamboo.

Foreword

The Plight of the Panda

There are about a thousand giant pandas left in western China. As this excellent account by Heather Angel makes clear, without a concerted international effort their prospects for survival in the wild look bleak.

As always, the threat comes from humans—in this case, extensive deforestation and habitat encroachment, combined with poaching. Some 50 percent of the habitat has been lost over the last twenty-five years, leaving the pandas confined to tiny isolated patches or reserves in a sea of humanity. Many of these reserves are too small to support genetically viable populations. In an overcrowded country like China, saving the panda will be an uphill struggle.

And the pandas don't make the situation any easier for themselves. With a digestive system of a carnivore—pandas will eat carrion given the chance—they have chosen instead to browse the bamboo that forms the understory of their forest habitat. As Heather shows, the consequence is that they are forced to spend most of their time feeding.

But this dietary specialization, combined with their fragmented distribution is now putting the pandas at even greater risk. About every fifty years, depending on the species, bamboo flowers, sets seed, and then dies. This flowering is synchronized over wide areas, resulting in large scale dieback of the panda's main food resource. In some of the smaller reserves, all the bamboos of a particular species may die, removing an essential component of their diet. In the past, pandas were forced to move on, and indeed this dispersion may have helped the genetic mix in an otherwise relatively sedentary population. But with humans now hemming in the reserves on all sides, the pandas have nowhere to go.

So how are the pandas to be saved? This is where the WWF becomes involved. In 1980, the WWF was the first outside conservation agency invited to work in China. A comprehensive survey of the panda population was undertaken, which led to the development with the Chinese Ministry of Forestry of a comprehensive "Conservation Programme for the Giant Panda and its Habitat," which now forms the basis for the future conservation of the species. Under the conservation program, the numbers of reserves will be doubled and "corridors," measuring approximately 0.6 miles (1 km) wide and planted with trees and bamboo, will be created to link reserves so that pandas can move between areas.

The total cost of this plan is a staggering $63.5 million. This is way beyond the capacity of the WWF alone to fund, and must depend upon support from the international community.

Despite this huge cost, the WWF has had some notable achievements to date through its own Panda Action Plan. The initial focus has been on the Minshan Region, which contains some 20 percent of the wild panda population. In Wanglang Reserve, equipment has been purchased, field research is underway, the population is being monitored, and patrols are trying to prevent illegal encroachment and poaching. This program has now been extended to include the network of some eleven reserves in the Minshan Mountains with an emphasis on staff training and field patrols. Integrated approaches are now being developed in Pingwu County, including around Wanglang, to put logging on a sustainable footing and identify alternative sources of income for local people.

Although this represents an excellent start, there is a mountain still to climb. We must improve the protection of the reserves both through increased patrolling and through education programs in the surrounding communities. Ultimately the fate of the panda rests in the hands of the local people—it is the role of the WWF by working with villages around the reserves, to show how nature conservation supports the development needs of the local people. We need to reconcile community development with the conservation of nature. In the long term, this is how we can secure a viable future for the panda.

The WWF is committed to helping the panda, and this book, with its marvelous photographs, gives you a glimpse of the wonder and beauty of the giant pandas in their natural habitat.

Robin Pellew
Director, WWF-UK

Introduction

A black-and-white shape shoots past me and shins up a tree. It disappears into the crown, but I can hear branches snapping and see them being tossed to the ground. Ten minutes later, the animal slides down the trunk like a firefighter down a pole. Landing unceremoniously with a thud on the forest floor, it rights itself and ambles off through the fern-rich undergrowth. All this happens so quickly, and in such poor light, that I fail to take a single picture of my first encounter with a giant panda. After eight trips to China, I can hardly believe that I am actually seeing this endearing, but, sadly, endangered, mammal in Sichuan's Qionglai Mountains.

As the panda disappears into the forest, I recall my first visit to Wolong, China's largest panda reserve, fourteen years ago. Early in May, the steep slopes were peppered with rhododendrons blooming among deciduous trees that were beginning to flush out with the exquisite green shades that herald the dawn of spring. Rhododendrons, not pandas, had been my primary objective in visiting this botanical paradise, which is a transitional zone between the severe Tibetan climate to the west and the warm Sichuan basin to the east. Precipitous slopes alternating with deep valleys contribute to the diversity of habitats in this species-rich area. The profusion of plant types provide food, shelter, and nest sites for countless birds and mammals, none more famous than the giant panda, which is almost totally dependent on a few kinds of bamboo for survival in this mountain refuge, one of the panda's last six ranges.

By the end of the first week in June, nearly all the deciduous trees have leafed out, uniting the patches of evergreen trees into a continuous green mantle. Looking up, I gain tantalizing glimpses of a high peak as the clouds part briefly. Wispy clouds spill over the lower peaks, waft in and out of ravines, and skirt behind bluffs, isolating individual trees on ridges and bringing a magical quality to this remote area so reminiscent of scenes in Chinese ink-brush paintings.

My thoughts turn to a French missionary, who, while drinking tea in a Sichuan hunter's hut in 1869, spotted the black-and-white skin of what he took to be a large bear. Yet, with such inhospitable terrain, almost half a century passed before a Westerner first saw a live giant panda. For a time, bagging a panda became the goal of big-game hunters; then, the race was on to collect a live animal for exhibition in the West. Late in 1936, when

A one-year-old panda sits astride a fallen tree trunk in the Wolong Reserve in Sichuan, China.

an American woman returning from China was photographed as she stepped ashore in San Francisco cradling a baby panda in her arms, the world's love affair with the charismatic creature began.

I mused that, although discovered well before the giant panda, the red panda—a smaller, raccoonlike animal with a long tail—has never evoked the same degree of affection. Today, few other animals are as revered as the giant panda, nor, indeed, are as popular and lucrative zoo exhibits. Once given as diplomatic gifts and always referred to by name in captivity, giant pandas are a cartoonist's dream, with their distinctive black-and-white markings, clownlike faces, and sooty eye patches. Young and old people alike are able to recognize a panda, even from a tiny reproduction of the WWF's international logo.

Despite arousing great affection among people the world over and being regarded as one of China's national treasures, the giant panda population has declined rapidly in the wild during this century, chiefly due to habitat destruction. All wildlife suffers from shrinking habitats, but for an animal that exists almost exclusively on a bamboo diet, the problem is exacerbated when most bamboo plants within an area flower at the same time and then die. I hope this book will help increase public awareness of the plight of the endangered giant and red pandas.

The black eye spots make the panda's eyes appear much larger than they actually are, lending the panda a clownlike face.

Swirling clouds—a feature of summers in Wolong—help maintain the region's moist environment.

In Search of the Giant Panda

A legend from Tibet, a vast mountainous region west of the Chinese province of Sichuan, explains how the giant panda gained its distinctive markings. Long ago, when pandas were completely white, a mother panda and her cub played with a shepherdess and her flock. Suddenly, a leopard attacked the cub, and the girl was killed while trying to defend it. Her courage so moved her three sisters and the pandas that they held a funeral for her, and, following the local custom, they covered their arms with ashes as a token of respect. As the pandas wept, they used their paws to wipe tears from their eyes and to cover their ears to deaden the sobs. The ashes blackened their eyes and ears.

Knowledge of the giant panda's existence outside China dates back to only 1869, yet a Chinese geography textbook from 2,500 years ago mentions a black-and-white bearlike animal. Indeed, the Chinese held the panda in high esteem in those times, for a panda skull was found in a royal tomb dating to 179 to 163 B.C. during the Western Han dynasty (206 B.C. to A.D. 24), when an emperor kept a giant panda along with a menagerie of rare animals in his garden at Xian, of Terracotta Army fame.

From the discovery of fossil remains, we know that the giant panda once existed over a much wider range, extending into Burma and northern Vietnam in the south, in China almost as far north as Beijing, the capital, and near Hong Kong and Shanghai to the east. Changes in climate reduced some of the panda's range, but in the twentieth century, the prime factor has been the rapid encroachment of the human population on the panda's habitat. As native forests have been logged or clear-cut for agriculture, suitable panda habitat has continued to shrink, until today it is confined to six mountain ranges running southwest from south of Xian to south of Chengdu along the eastern edge of the Tibetan plateau.

The Western world was first alerted to the giant panda's existence by the French missionary Père Armand David in 1869. He initially thought he had discovered a new kind of carnivore, which he named *Ursus melanoleucus*—"the black-and-white bear." But after Professor Alphonse Milne-Edwards, a French zoologist, examined panda specimens sent to him by Père David, he realized the skeleton and teeth showed affinities closer to the red panda and, hence, to raccoons. In 1870, the giant panda was renamed *Ailuropoda melanoleuca*, meaning

Framed by bamboo, a giant panda walks along a snow-covered track in February. Standing on all fours, a giant panda adopts a bearlike stance.

"pandalike black-and-white animal." Zoologists have continued to debate whether the giant panda has more bearlike or raccoonlike characteristics; some believe it should be classified in its own family, quite distinct from bears or raccoons.

Even though Père David spent many months attempting to obtain a live giant panda, he had to be content with dead animals or their skins, brought to him by hunters. Despite several plant-hunting expeditions scouring mountainous parts of Sichuan for attractive plants of interest to the western horticultural world, none brought sight of a giant panda. However, the inhospitable terrain and the dense bamboo understory could easily have hidden what, even by then, was a rare animal. By 1913, although no foreigner had yet seen a live panda, skins commanded a high price in Chengdu, where Europeans used them as floor rugs.

Tree-like rhododendron flowers on Mount Emei in Sichuan, where pandas lived as recently as 1948.

The first sighting by a Westerner of a live giant panda was made by German zoologist Hugo Weigold in 1916. However, this turned out not to be a wild animal but a young panda purchased from local people. Unfortunately, all attempts by Weigold at hand-rearing failed, and the animal died shortly afterward.

Nonetheless, proof that the giant panda still roamed the mountainous habitat fired the imagination of big-game hunters. Having the right connections certainly helped U.S. President Theodore Roosevelt's sons—Theodore Jr. and Kermit—to stage the 1928–1929 expedition to China, sponsored by Chicago's Field Museum of Natural History. The expedition was eventually rewarded by panda droppings and tracks in the snow. On April 13, 1929, the two brothers shot simultaneously and bagged the first giant panda. As news filtered back to the West, other museums became eager to sponsor hunters so they, too, could have their own stuffed panda as a novel exhibit. Zoos were also quick to appreciate that a live giant panda would be a huge attraction.

The story of how the first live panda reached the West reads more like fiction than reality. The main character was the newly wed Ruth Harkness, a petite New York fashion designer. When her husband died in

Deep in winter, snow falls on the Wolong, when waterfalls also freeze.

Shanghai shortly after their marriage, Harkness was determined to carry out his dream of collecting a live panda for New York City's Bronx Zoo. So, in 1936, she left for China.

All the people Harkness met in China, including one of her late husband's colleagues, whom she described as "Zoology" Jones, advised her not to proceed. After all, Jones had hunted the country for nearly two decades and had never set eyes on a giant panda. At that time, it was also unwise for foreign women to travel alone in China. In Jones's opinion, the odds of Harkness even sighting a panda were one in a million.

Then she met Quentin Young, an American-born Chinese hunter, who agreed to be her expedition leader. The necessary food, medicines, camping and cooking equipment, tools, guns and ammunition, and five traps for capturing adult pandas were duly assembled. At the eleventh hour, Harkness bought a nursing bottle, nipples, and some dried milk powder.

Throughout winter, corn cobs hang outside farm houses in the valley of the Wolong Reserve, and during the Chinese New Year in late January or February, the doors are decorated.

The expedition left Shanghai on September 26, 1936, and sailed up the Yangtze River to Chengdu, the capital of Sichuan Province. The group then walked from Chengdu to Wenchuan. Moving up into the Qionglai Mountains, they crossed rivers on swaying bamboo bridges to a site within the area now designated as the Wolong Reserve, passing rooftops golden with drying corn along the way. To illustrate the difficulty of the expedition's task, not even the local people could agree on the size of a *bei-shung*—the local name for the giant panda. Estimates ranged from as "big as a horse" to as "small as a dog." By the time the expedition reached its final camp early in November, the trees covering the hills around the valley were bedecked in flaming autumnal colors and the hot days were interspersed with cold nights.

A panda feeds on bamboo during mid-winter.

Père Armand David

The rose species Rosa davidii *was one of many plants discovered in China's Sichuan Province by Père Armand David, the first Westerner to describe the giant panda.*

We owe much to Père Armand David's acute observations and collections. Many of the plant and animal specimens he recorded in China were named after him. Among these are Père David's deer *(Elephurus davidiensis)* and a tree called the Chinese dove, or pocket-handkerchief *(Davidia involucrata)*, which bears conspicuous white bracts resembling doves or handkerchiefs fluttering in the breeze. The butterfly bush *(Buddleia davidii)*, with fragrant purple flowering spikes that attract butterflies, also originates from China. Less well known is the attractive species rose *(Rosa davidii)*, a wild rose that bears clusters of from five to twelve deep pink flowers.

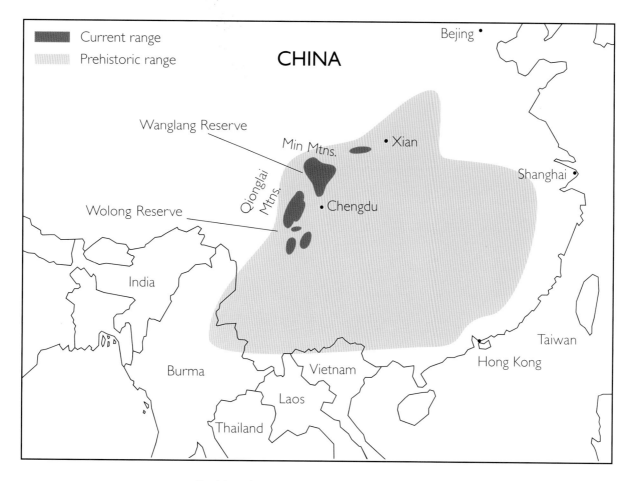

Prehistoric and current range of the giant panda

By the time it is a year old, a panda is adept at climbing trees.

As Harkness trekked through the dense bamboo forests, negotiating fallen tree trunks and taking care not to slip down the perpendicular gulleys, she began to ponder why she had not stayed in New York designing purple velvet tea gowns. But such thoughts were instantly banished from her mind when the expedition found some giant panda droppings. In Harkness's own words, "Pure gold couldn't have been more exciting." From their final camp, the expedition made daily trips to build log bridges over raging icy torrents so they could reach remote areas for trapping. By this time, snow had begun to fall around the camp, and Harkness was moved to write, "a stranger thing I have never seen than snow on green bamboo."

There is some doubt as to who captured the first live panda. Harkness's story is that, although the hunters had been briefed not to shoot a panda, one of them attempted to fire at a female. She fled, and shortly thereafter, the hunters heard a whimpering sound from within a rotten tree trunk. Harkness described the moment she caught up to Quentin Young: "There in the palm of his two hands was a squirming baby bei-shung." It was a race against time to get the baby panda back to camp where it could be fed. Harkness decided to call her new charge Su Lin, which means "a little bit of something very cute."

The youngster, which weighed no more than 3 pounds (1.36 kilograms) and still had its eyes closed, was quoted as being ten days old. This seems unlikely, since a newborn panda weighs between 2.6 and 5.3 ounces (75 to 150 grams) and is naked; the characteristic black-and-white panda pattern doesn't fully develop until twenty days. Furthermore, wild panda cubs are normally born in late August or early September. Pictures of Su Lin taken in Shanghai two weeks after her capture suggest she was at least two months old.

In her account of the journey, Harkness writes that she "felt like a young and incompetent mother with her first baby." She fed Su Lin on demand every six or seven hours, and the sole feeding bottle had to be guarded carefully as the expedition descended the mountain carrying the panda in a green bamboo basket. By the time Harkness and Su Lin arrived in Shanghai, news of the capture was spreading like wildfire. Their departure from China was chaotic.

The Chinese characters for giant panda. In descending order, the characters read: "big bear cat."

23

Harkness describes how "panda-monium" broke out in the Shanghai Customs House when Su Lin could not feed because the nipple on the bottle was too small.

As Harkness stepped ashore in San Francisco cradling Su Lin in her arms, the press were ecstatic with the story of how she had succeeded in her quest, where many beefier men before her had failed. Inevitably, some of the more chauvinist elements of the press cast doubts on exactly how she had acquired Su Lin. Even so, when Harkness eventually arrived back in New York, just a few days before Christmas, she and Su Lin were much feted. Indeed, they were invited to the thirty-third annual banquet of the New York Explorer's Club; no woman had ever attended this all-male function before, let alone been guest of honor!

American Ruth Harkness was amazed to see green bamboo covered with snow during her 1936 visit to Sichuan in search of pandas.

After all her efforts to secure a live giant panda, Harkness was dismayed when the Bronx Zoo rejected Su Lin, fearful of the problems it might encounter in its attempts to rear a giant panda. Harkness eventually offered Su Lin to Brookfield Zoo in Chicago, where the panda was a star exhibit from February 8, 1937, until her sudden death on April 1, 1938, when she choked on a piece of wood. This tragic accident took place just six weeks after Harkness returned from a second trip to China with a potential mate for Su Lin. Only after Su Lin had died was it discovered that she was, in fact, a male!

Zoos throughout the world began to clamor for a giant panda. During the next decade, fifteen more giant pandas left China for exhibition in western zoos; two of the animals died before arrival. Ming was one of several pandas that came to London. She was regarded with such affection by the British public that when she died on December 26, 1944, Ming had the distinction of her obituary appearing in the *Times* of London. Throughout the history of the London Zoo, no other animal had so touched the imagination of young and old, alike.

In later years, zoos outside China began to cooperate with each other, loaning giant pandas in an attempt to mate them. But on the rare occasions when a successful mating took place and a cub was born, it survived only briefly.

Occasionally, giant pandas were given as diplomatic gifts; during U.S. President Richard Nixon's 1972 visit to China, he was presented with a pair of pandas—Ling Ling (female) and Hsing Hsing (male) for the National Zoo in Washington. In 1983, Ling Ling became pregnant, but her baby died three hours after it was born, and the following year Ling Ling gave birth to a stillborn cub. After the Chinese government placed a ban on the permanent export of pandas in 1982, the few remaining zoos with pandas discovered they had an exhibit with even greater power to draw the public.

For a time, pandas were loaned for special occasions, such as Australia's bicentenary, but conservationists objected to the use of pandas captured from the wild for short-term loans, because the wild population is so vulnerable. Despite such concerns, in September 1996 a pair of pandas—Bai-Yun,

Growing at 8,300 feet (2,520 meters) elevation, the leaves on a snow-covered rhododendron become tightly enrolled and hang down after a cold night.

a captive-bred five-year-old female, and Shi-Shi, an older male rescued injured from the wild—was loaned to the Zoological Society of San Diego for a twelve-year period. This, the biggest rent-a-panda deal to date, requires the zoo to contribute $1 million annually to aid wild habitat protection projects in China and to assist with the training of Chinese scientists. Any cubs born to the panda pair at San Diego will belong to China.

Home and Habits

The home of the giant panda is almost idyllic. Pandas live in a forest with comfortable temperatures that are neither too hot in summer nor too cold in winter and a rich array of deciduous and coniferous trees and a plentiful food supply close at hand. Regardless of the season, colorful pheasants wander in and out of this scene, which is enlivened in spring by blooming rhododendrons and in autumn by fiery hues. Familiar sights and sounds have persisted for centuries, as successive generations of pandas reared their offspring in this mountain haven.

Then one day, the natural sounds were drowned by the noise of huge trees crashing to the floor. Humans had moved in to extract the forest giants. At the lower altitudes, farmers were clearing the natural forest and terracing the slopes to plant corn and other crops. The panda's home was threatened.

Pictures taken by satellite show that the panda habitat in Sichuan shrunk by half between 1974 and 1989. Pandas are now confined to mountains in just three Chinese provinces—Sichuan, Gansu, and Shaanxi—along the eastern flank of the Tibetan plateau. Pandas live at altitudes between 7,500 and 10,830 feet (2,300 and 3,300 meters), moving up to cooler elevations in summer and back down in winter, descending even farther down the mountains in severe weather. These zones offer a relatively mild, wet climate with plenty of moisture from rain in summer and snow in winter to nurture the growth of bamboo.

At the end of the nineteenth century, the steep slopes rising up from the valley of the Pitiao River—a remote area in southwestern Sichuan's Qionglai Mountains—were still clothed in a variety of forests. Twenty thousand years ago, these forests had survived the last Ice Age because the high peaks had held back advancing glaciers. The area was special for its great variety of plants and animals—some found nowhere else in the world. Animals that shared the giant panda's home included red pandas, clouded leopards, golden monkeys, musk deer, takins (goatlike antelopes with a golden coat), and several kinds of colorful pheasants. It was an area of high biodiversity.

Tibetan farmers began to settle in the region in the early twentieth century. They cut trees on lower slopes to supply timber to build homes, provide firewood, and clear the land for growing crops. When commercial logging commenced in 1916, only large, single conifers were cut from within forests high in the mountains, but

A panda browses on bamboo against a mountain backdrop.

by the time logging reached its peak, between 1966 and 1973, large areas had been clear-cut.

Without a canopy of trees, the scrubby undergrowth took over, forming a dense ground cover. This not only made it difficult for giant pandas to move with ease, but also created unfavorable conditions for bamboo seedlings to flourish. By the mid-1970s, the region's rich flora and fauna were severely threatened. A 1974 census revealed that Wolong supported the highest density of giant pandas in Sichuan. The following year, the area was declared a natural reserve and logging was halted. In 1980, Wolong was designated a man and biosphere reserve, and the Chinese government and WWF set up a research and conservation center for the giant panda at Hetauping within the reserve.

In late summer, a waterfall plunges down a rock face into the Pitiao River. By midwinter, the waterfall will freeze.

On a clear day in the reserve, you can see bands of different forest types for each vegetation zone moving up the mountainsides from the Pitiao Valley. Along the Pitiao River, at an elevation of 5,250 to 6,560 feet (1,600 to 2,000 meters), the forest is a mix of evergreen and deciduous broad-leaved trees. In spring, these deciduous trees flush out in varied hues of green or bronze that gradually merge into an overall somber green as spring fades into summer. In autumn, the lower slopes in the reserve transform into a kaleidoscope of hot colors. By the time the leaves fall in early winter to reveal the bare brown branches, these slopes become drab. Then, an overnight snowfall etches the shape of bare trunks and branches with a white layer that separates them from the evergreens as graphic, monochromatic sculptured forms. Within a few hours, snow transforms the valley into a winter wonderland.

Snow falls frequently in the Pitiao Valley during February, but once the sun beams directly onto the lower slopes the magical scene melts away, in contrast to the forests cloaked by a permanent white winter envelope in the cooler air above. For this reason, I cherish the days when a thick cloud cover curtains out the sun so that the

Even when only a year old, a giant panda is adept at climbing large trees, such as this pine.

glistening white mantle persisted in the valley. Come afternoon, the clouds descended from the peaks and obliterated the upper slopes, which I longed to explore. So when the opportunity arose for me to climb up to 8,300 feet (2,530 meters), I grasped it with both hands. My destination is Wuyipeng, a research area established in 1978, where zoologist Dr. George Schaller led Chinese colleagues in pioneering fieldwork into the panda's habits and way of life.

My journey begins in a smoke-filled room in a local farmer's house, where hams hang from the ceiling, curing above a log fire. Here, my Chinese guide, Huang Yan, recruits two farmers to be our porters. Almost immediately, we cross the Pitiao River via a cable bridge that swings in an unnerving manner with every step. I begin to sense how Ruth Harkness must have felt when she journeyed into the Qionglai Mountains more than half a century ago. As we climb higher, the shallow wooden steps are buried beneath snow, making it impossible to gauge where to step with any degree of safety.

Once we ascend beyond the lower slopes, the vegetation becomes still more varied. Among the conifers are rhododendrons—ranging from small shrubs to large trees—that flower from May onward. At 7,220 feet (2,200 meters), birch and fir trees begin to appear among the clumps of umbrella bamboo. Close to the camp we spot fresh tracks from an Asiatic golden cat, but otherwise—apart from a few birdcalls—there is little visible or audible evidence of wildlife. Most of the climb is steep, so it is a relief when the last lap of

Golden monkeys share the forests in Wolong with the giant panda. Here a mother cradles a youngster.

the trail levels out and skirts a valley hugging the mountain. In places, umbrella bamboo on either side arch over the narrow path, forming a virtual tunnel. As we approach Wuyipeng, the rhododendrons are noticeably larger. Lacy gray ropes of epiphytic lichens festoon many trees, and the sun shines on birches with large cinnamon-colored sheets of flaking bark, so that the bark glows as vibrantly as any autumnal leaves.

As I round the last corner and face the huts at Wuyipeng, I see their roofs decorated with two-foot (60-cm) icicles—proof that the daytime temperatures temporarily rise above freezing. On our first afternoon,

Two tree trunks close together provide a convenient gap in which a panda can wedge its body.

snow begins to fall at 2:30 P.M. and continues throughout the night. Walking in the fresh snow at dawn the next morning, I sense an ethereal silence, punctuated only by the occasional call of a tragopan pheasant and the periodic *rat-tat-tat* of a woodpecker at work.

Bamboo flourishes within the shade of the forest, where groves comprise much of the understory. Seven species of bamboo grow in the Wolong Reserve, but only two are of prime importance as food for pandas. At lower elevations of 5,250 to 8,790 feet (1,600 to 2,680 meters), umbrella bamboo *(Fargesia robusta)* dominates; higher up at 7,550 to 11,810 feet (2,300 to 3,600 meters), the less-robust arrow bamboo *(Bashania fangiana)* is most widespread. Around Wuyipeng, the two species grow alongside one another. With bamboo groves surrounding the camp, I have high hopes of finding some evidence of a giant panda—either from bamboo fragments or fresh droppings—but none was sighted during the three days I spent at Wuyipeng.

Trees beside Narrow Lake in Jiuzhaigou Reserve, Sichuan Province, provide a study in gold and aquamarine.

Walking the mountain paths used by the researchers was precarious. The trail mostly followed the edge of a precipitous slope. Any ravine or stream that cut into the mountainside was bridged simply by saplings lashed together. Wherever the overhead canopy blocked out the warming rays from the sun, knee-deep snow hid holes and fallen trunks.

Around 8,200 feet (2,500 meters), snow accumulates on stones within streambeds, but water continues to flow throughout the winter and, apart from occasional birdcalls, the splashy gurgles provide a welcome sound against the stillness of calm days within the forest.

On days when the sun shines brightly, the sounds of melting snow also break the stillness. Then, gentle tinkling sounds echo through the forest as snow falls from the conifer crowns onto dead leaves wedged in branches. Periodically, a sunbeam sparkles as a myriad of minute icy shards rain down from the branches. In places where snow-covered rocks are warmed by the sun, the dripping water refreezes each night, eventually glazing the rocks with impressive ice curtains. Elsewhere, daggerlike icicles frame cave entrances, and ice stalactites grow down from the ceilings inside.

Within the Min Mountains, nearly 300 miles (480 kilometers) northeast of Wolong, lies another panda reserve reached by a tortuous road, frequently blocked by landslides. Jiuzhaigou, or Nine Village Gorge, has to be one of the most beautiful locations in China. Hidden within a remote mountain region, the area was known only to the local inhabitants until Chinese foresters stumbled upon the fairyland in the 1970s. Two decades later, the United Nations Educational, Scientific, and Cultural Organization (UNESCO) declared it a world heritage site.

As encrustations build up on fallen trees in the crystal blue water of Five Flower Lake in Jiuzhaigou, the trees take on a ghostly appearance.

What makes Jiuzhaigou so special? It is not the bamboo, which is so essential for pandas, but the exceptional landscapes that make it unique. Situated along an 18.6-mile (30-km) stretch at an elevation of 6,560 to 10,170 feet (2,000 to 3,100 meters), rivers, waterfalls, streams, and a series of alpine lakes (108 in all) adorn the high mountains plunging into deep valleys. Various minerals dissolved within the waters create a palette of colors from one lake to the next, ranging from deep blue, turquoise, and emerald to amber. The mineral deposits also preserve submerged fallen trees. Broad, shallow rivers flow through the gorge, and, in places where the steep slope flattens out, myriad miniature islands dotted with small trees punctuate the watery expanse formed by these rivers, creating a so-called potted landscape. In late June, the hillsides come alive with rhododendron blooms of varied hues, and in the autumn, the mixed forest becomes a patchwork of vibrant colors backed by evergreen conifers and snowcapped peaks.

Sadly, these unique qualities, which have resulted in Jiuzhaigou's meteoric recognition, may well be the gorge's undoing. Pressure from tourism is great, and, unless action is taken to prevent people from swarming over the carbonate terraces and leaving rubbish in their wake, the fragile qualities will be short-lived. As Jiuzhaigou is Sichuan's prime tourist attraction, the situation can only become exacerbated.

Within Jiuzhaigou, Wolong, and other isolated mountainous areas, giant pandas lead essentially solitary lives. Each panda has a home range—an area where it spends most of its life—covering 1.5 to 2.5 square miles (3.9 to 6.4 sq km). The males generally have a larger home range than the females, who tend to remain in smaller core areas. Female pandas select their home range on west-facing slopes with a gentle incline, where the snow melts more quickly. They also look for an area with a hollow tree or cave to serve as a potential den site. They will not tolerate other females encroaching into their central core area. The outer fringes of their core areas often overlap with those of other males and females.

A proud Chang minority mother with her twins. The family lives in the heart of panda country in the Wolong Reserve.

Pandas have neither the time nor the energy to defend their ground, so they just mark their home ranges by squatting on the ground or backing up against a tree or a rock and rubbing their rear portions to deposit secretions from the anal gland, often using their tail as a brush. They may also use urine to scent mark, in which case the deposit has a strong musky odor. Most often pandas mark at their shoulder height, but occasionally they have been seen to scent mark higher up a tree by doing a handstand and walking backward up the trunk. Objects used as scent posts have a dark area rubbed smooth with claw marks above. During the breeding season, scent marks function like calling cards by relaying the reproductive state of an individual panda. When a female is in heat, she marks more frequently to ensure a male is attracted to her at the right time. Adult males scent mark more often than either females or young pandas. Males continue to territory mark outside the breeding season.

Young pandas, as well as weak individuals, sometimes fall prey to leopards or packs of wild Asian dogs, or dholes. A healthy adult panda can escape by disappearing into a bamboo thicket, by swimming across a river, or by climbing a tree. If attempts to escape fail, then powerful blows with paws tipped with sharp claws are usually an effective deterrent to any predator.

The flat-footed waddling gait of pandas belies their agile ability to climb. To ascend a tree, pandas hug the trunk with their forearms, while their claws help secure their grip. Youngsters may climb to escape from predators. In colder weather, pandas warm themselves by ascending to a sunspot above the shady forest floor.

The giant panda has many adaptations for life in its environment. When making a rapid descent from a tree, the panda's thick pelt helps cushion a hard fall. The coarse, oily hairs on its coat are an effective barrier to water and snow in the year-round humid atmosphere. After a rain or snow shower, I have seen a panda shake itself to remove excess water. Like bears and large cats, pandas groom their coats and muddy paws by licking them clean. In common with polar bears, the soles of panda paws are covered with hair to insulate the pads when walking on snow. Sharp claws on all four feet enable pandas not only to grip tree trunks but also to scratch, to strip bark, to mark trees, and to manipulate bamboo stems while feeding. Sitting in an evenly lit clearing among green vegetation, the black-and-white body of a panda is very conspicuous; yet when it walks in dappled light, its body outline is disrupted as black patches merge into shadowy areas.

Devoting time and money to save the panda's misty, mountain home will ensure not only that one of the world's most appealing animals has a reasonable chance of survival, but also that the rich flora and fauna associated with this special region will be saved. There is still much to learn about the panda's biology and behavior, yet sparse populations coupled with a precipitous habitat make it difficult for researchers to study more than a few individuals in one area. Zoologists at San Diego Zoo are studying the pair of pandas they have on loan to determine whether scientists can detect information about the gender, age, and reproductive state of pandas from their scent marks. If it is proved that individual pandas can be identified in this way, future field surveys could be based on an analysis of their scent, rather than on tracking the elusive animals themselves. This would not only save researchers' time, but also minimize disturbance to the pandas, since they would not have to be fitted with radio collars.

The Need to Feed

The varied foods associated with different regions of the world contribute to the delights of traveling abroad. Imagine, then, the tedium of being a giant panda and necessarily spending more than half of every twenty-four-hour period consuming one type of plant simply to stay alive. Even though pandas are known to eat several kinds of wild plants, bamboo still comprises more than 99 percent of their diet. Just why the giant panda has become so dependent on bamboo has long puzzled scientists. It may be simply that the evergreen plants are plentiful and nearly always available.

Fossil remains indicate that the panda was originally a carnivore that gradually became herbivorous, turning to a diet of the bamboo that thrives in the forest understory. As the panda began to eat more bamboo and less meat, its body gradually adapted to a less active life, making it less capable of hunting down prey. Present day pandas, however, still appreciate the chance to eat carrion. They have been known to scavenge on discarded bones; indeed, scientists use meat as bait to lure pandas into live traps. Zoologist George Schaller found golden monkey hair in one panda dropping, and the hair, bones, and hooves of musk deer in another.

Bamboo groves develop within the shade of the forest on the more gently sloping parts of the steep mountains. The groves fail to flourish in areas where the forests have been clear-cut, because bamboo seedlings shrivel and die when exposed to sun. Giant pandas will feed on several different kinds of bamboo, but in each location they show a distinct preference for one or two species. In Wolong, which has a monsoon climate with most of the 47.25 inches (1,200 millimeters) of annual rainfall falling between April and November, two kinds of bamboo are favored by the giant panda. Umbrella bamboo grows much taller and forms much denser clumps than the slender arrow bamboo preferred by the red panda. In summer and autumn, the giant panda selects the leaves of arrow bamboo, ignoring the slender new stems; whereas by winter, year-old stems and leaves are eaten, as well as the leaves of umbrella bamboo. In May and June the pandas move down the mountain to feed on fresh umbrella bamboo shoots breaking through the ground. The shoots contain more moisture and protein than stems or mature leaves.

The amount of time a panda is active and the distance it travels each day can be determined by tracking

When feeding on bamboo leaves, a panda amasses a bunch at one side of its mouth.

an animal fitted with a radio collar. To fit the collar, researchers must first entice the panda into a harmless trap and briefly tranquilize it so that the fitting will neither upset the panda nor risk the safety of the handlers. From tracking the radio collars, Schaller and his researchers at Wolong have found that a panda is active for about fourteen hours a day. Most of this time is spent feeding within a small range. On average, this involves moving

The panda uses its tongue to manipulate the bamboo leaves inside its mouth.

1,640 feet (500 meters) per day; but if food is plentiful, it may be less. When searching for new umbrella bamboo shoots in spring, a panda may travel up to 4,920 feet (1,500 meters) per day. Schaller and his researchers calculated that to maintain enough energy to go about its daily routine—including walking to find food, feeding, drinking, defecating, grooming, and scent marking—a panda must feed for more than twelve hours in every twenty-four-hour period. There were two distinct activity peaks—one at dawn, and another in late afternoon. After gorging itself, the giant panda rests, usually for two to four hours. By the time it awakes, the panda has voided large droppings containing poorly digested bamboo fragments, and it is ready to begin feeding again.

Feeding strategies adopted by the giant panda depend on the time of year and whether it is feeding on new or old shoots. Before feeding, a panda may sniff a bamboo clump to see if it is worth eating, then it sits down with its hind legs stretched out in front of its body. The panda manipulates a bamboo cane with great dexterity by using its enlarged wrist bone, which functions as a sixth digit—the so-called thumb. This pseudothumb can be moved up against the first finger in a pincerlike movement to hold and maneuver a bamboo stem.

Pandas have teeth that closely mirror the dentition of a typical carnivore; however, their teeth have become modified for prolonged chewing of woody plants. Sharply pointed canines effectively slice through the woody bamboo stems, but pandas lack the carnassial teeth used by carnivores to cut meat. Flattened,

To aid in eating the bamboo, the panda grips the cane with its fingers and pseudothumb.

well-developed premolar teeth with many cusps function like molars to provide additional force for crushing and grinding coarse bamboo. Unlike red pandas, giant pandas give each mouthful only a cursory chew, but massive jaw and cheekbones, as well as oversized chewing muscles attached to the greatly enlarged cranium and teeth, aid prolonged periods of chewing. A leathery gullet and a thick-walled stomach combined with heavy mucus secretions ensure that the panda's gut is not injured by the passage of sharp-edged bamboo splinters.

Pandas differ from typical herbivores in having retained the simple stomach and short gut characteristic of a carnivore. Once swallowed, bamboo passes quickly through a panda. Using carrots as a colored marker, food took eight hours, on average, to pass through the gut of captive pandas at Washington Zoo. Pandas lack micro-organisms in their gut to break down plant cell walls by a fermentation process, so, unlike ruminants, such as sheep and cattle, pandas cannot digest much of the food they eat. This means that the panda has to consume huge amounts of bamboo just to stay alive. A panda may continue to feed and defecate as it walks through the forest.

Because the nutritional value of bamboo is so low, a giant panda—unlike many bears—is unable to lay down fat reserves to allow it to hibernate. Interestingly, when captive pandas are given a protein-rich diet, they tend to gain weight and even become obese. Dependent on a daily supply of fresh bamboo, a wild panda cannot hoard food, either. Instead, it forages day in and day out on bamboo, which is present throughout the year.

Schaller and his research team used several methods to estimate the amount of bamboo consumed each day by an adult panda. By weighing the droppings produced from a known amount of fresh bamboo eaten by a captive panda, they calculated the amount of food eaten from the droppings produced by a wild panda over a similar time span. They also estimated the amount of food consumed in the wild by counting the number of stems eaten and deducting from this figure the amount of bamboo debris strewn along the track. They calculated that for most of the year, an adult panda consumes 22 to 40 pounds (10 to 18 kilograms) of bamboo leaves and stems per day, and up to twice as much in spring. At this time of year, the new, succulent shoots contain so much water that pandas don't have to expend energy traveling to a stream or river to drink. During the rest of the year, because streams are numerous in the mountainous habitat, pandas have no trouble finding water. Even in the depths of winter, when streambed rocks are obliterated by several inches of snow, I could hear the water gurgling in every valley stream I crossed at Wuyipeng.

For several decades, a bamboo clump flourishes and increases girth by sending out creeping under-

A panda feeds on bamboo in winter. A cane is held in one or both forepaws while the leaf clusters are bitten off and retained in one corner of the mouth. When the bunch is a reasonable size, it is removed from the mouth and eaten.

After an overnight snowfall, bamboo leaves become thickly encrusted with snow, but as a panda bites through the stem and brings the cane up to its mouth, most of the snow falls to the ground.

ground stems or rhizomes, from which spring new shoots. As a result, pandas never have to travel far to feed. Like all flowering plants, however, the only way bamboo can disperse through the forest and maintain its genetic diversity is to produce seeds. Bamboos are unusual grasses that flower at infrequent intervals. Depending on the species, this may be anywhere from once every decade to once a century. After flowering, the bamboos set seed, then die. This synchronous flowering followed by death opens up parts of the forest for tree saplings to invade. Later on, these, in turn, provide the prerequisite shade for bamboo groves to develop.

In the past, when the natural forest was more extensive, bamboo dieback did not present a major hardship to pandas. It may, in fact, have had a beneficial effect by forcing pandas to move farther afield to feed, thereby bringing new genetic material into otherwise isolated panda populations. As logging and the spread of agriculture broke up the forest into smaller, separate fragments, pandas became restricted to smaller areas. If these areas contained only a single palatable bamboo species, then bamboo dieback began to have serious consequences. Faced with the uniformity of a landscape altered by humans, few pandas ventured into new feeding areas. While some turned to alternative food plants, many failed to eat enough to sustain life and died. In Wanglang Reserve (south of Jiuzhaigou in the Min Mountains) a panda population estimated at 196 individuals in 1969 had dropped to fewer than 20 in 1980.

In locations where more than one kind of palatable bamboo is present, few pandas starve to death. There is also no problem when the flowering periods are staggered at different altitudes, so that the plants at one level recover by the time plants at another level begin to die off. For instance, in 1976, a mass die-off of umbrella bamboo occurred in Jiuzhaigou Reserve at elevations between 8,530 and 10,500 feet (2,600 and 3,200 meters). At lower elevations, however, the umbrella bamboo did not flower until several years later, when bamboo from the previous die-off had been reestablished. When the flowering periods are staggered in this way, pandas are able to respond simply by moving up or down the mountainside.

By restricting itself to one kind of food, the giant panda becomes vulnerable when its food supply suddenly plummets. If the animal is unable to migrate elsewhere to feed, it starves to death, since new bamboo plants can take up to two decades to provide a sustainable food source.

The panda's dentition is more like that of a carnivore than a typical herbivore.

To help conserve energy, a panda may lie down to feed.

Breeding and Survival

Not all mammals give birth to cute, cuddly offspring. In fact, it would be hard to find a less-appealing cub than the tiny pink object produced by a giant panda. But after about three months, the underdeveloped newborn becomes transformed into an enchanting youngster with a somewhat oversized head in relation to its body. On a cold February morning in Wolong, I was invited to view the most recent arrival at the breeding center. It took a few moments for my eyes to adjust to the dim light. Then, there in the corner of the enclosure I saw the cutest monochromatic bundle I have ever seen—a five-month-old panda cub.

Wild pandas become sexually mature at five-and-a-half to six-and-a-half years old and seek out partners in the spring, when they become more vocal. At that time of year, barks, bleats, and roars resonate through the forest, especially when two animals meet. Male pandas may even broadcast their presence farther afield by climbing a tree and barking from aloft. Scent marks are also used more extensively during the breeding season, enabling males to locate their potential mates within the dense forest.

During the twelve to twenty-five days the female panda is in heat, she produces a curious bleating sound not unlike a sheep. If she attracts several males, a confrontation may arise between two competing suitors. Without a pliable, expressive face, a panda has to depend on body posture to communicate. The dominant male signals his superiority by staring at his rival with his head lowered so that his black ears stand out clearly against the white fur behind. This may be followed by head bobbing and a swat with a forepaw. Occasionally, a confrontation may escalate into one animal biting an opponent's neck or head if the opportunity arises. An intimidated panda will adopt a submissive posture by lowering its head and covering its eyes with its forepaws. A male must approach a prospective mate with caution; if he moves in before her brief one-to-three-day receptive period, he may be given a sharp blow with a paw. An unresponsive female may also retreat up a tree to escape a persistent suitor.

Mating takes place from mid-March to mid-May. When ready to mate, the female adopts a submissive posture by crouching on the ground with her head lowered or even tucked tightly into her chest, and she presents her rear as she walks backward toward a male. As he mounts her, he places his forepaws on her back.

A meeting of two pandas in the Wolong Reserve.

An eighteen-month-old panda climbs a tree.

A female may mate with several males and may mate several times with one animal. After mating, it takes anywhere from one to three-and-a-half months for the fertilized embryo to be implanted in the mother's uterus, where it begins to develop. This is not a feature unique to pandas; badgers also have delayed implantation. Irrespective of the mating date, one, two, or, very rarely, three cubs are born usually in late August or early September.

After mating, the male takes no further part in rearing its young. A few days before she gives birth, the female seeks out a hollow tree or cave as her den—preferably near a natural water source. Removal of larger trees from some forests means that potential den sites—which must have cavities large enough for the mother to fit in easily when sitting—are now scarce. Once the mother locates a suitable den, she lines it with branches and bamboo leaves in preparation for the new offspring. The tiny pink newborn panda cub has a conspicuous tail, one-third the length of its body. At birth, its skin is covered with a white lanugo coat, without any trace of the distinctive black-and-white markings. Blind at birth, this infant weighs only about 2.6 to 5.3 ounces (75 to 150 grams)—a mere 0.11 percent of its mother's weight.

Continuous video monitoring allows biologists to study the early development of a young panda in captivity without interfering with the mother and her offspring. The infant's vocalizations are also recorded. A mother takes infinite care of her newborn cub. Should twin cubs be born, however, the mother rarely rears both. Normally, only the firstborn survives. The other is usually abandoned and either starves to death or becomes accidentally crushed beneath the weight of the mother's body. After giving birth, the mother gently cradles the infant to her chest with a forepaw so it can suckle. Even when not feeding, the infant is held in this position or beneath its mother's chin where it gains warmth and protection. In the early stages, the youngster is so small it is easily hidden by its mother's paw and fur. For the first few days, the mother doesn't leave the den at all. She eats nothing and sleeps very little. If she doses off and relaxes her grip, the baby can accidentally fall to the ground, in which case it complains loudly until picked up. It was thought a mother stayed with her cub for up to six days before she left to feed, but the Chinese scientists Professor Pan Wenshi and Dr. Lu Zhi studied a mother in the Qinling Mountains that remained with her newborn for twenty-five days, neither feeding nor defecating through-out this time. As the baby develops, the mother leaves it for short periods to forage and drink.

A female panda uses her mouth to hold, clean, or move her infant. If danger threatens, a mother may move her cub to a new den site. During the first month, a mother licks her infant's backside to stimulate defecation. She then eats the droppings to keep the den clean, thereby reducing the chance of attracting predators, such as the yellow-throated marten. In addition to frequently nursing her newborn, the mother also licks it up to fifteen times a day to keep it clean, to prevent the bare skin from drying out, and to provide immunity. She continues to clean her infant until it is one year old.

When the baby is a week old, ghostly black patches begin to show on the ears. A few days later, the skin around the eyes and on the legs begins to darken. By twenty days, the distinctive monochromatic markings are clearly visible. After four to seven weeks, the mother carries her cub around so it remains close by her as she feeds. The eyes open fully after six to seven weeks, when the panda cub begins to crawl. After three months, the cub begins to take its first hesitant steps, and by five months it can trot along beside its mother when she makes her feeding forays. Many cubs found curled up in the fork of a tree thought to have been abandoned by their mothers have misguidedly been rescued and transferred to captive breeding centers. Pan Wenshi has since discovered that a mother will leave her cub for up to fifty hours while she goes off to feed.

From the fork of a tree, a young panda surveys a snowy scene within the forest.

In the wild, a panda cub begins to feed on bamboo when it is five to six months old and is weaned after another three months. By the time it is one-and-a-half years old, the youngster is no longer dependent on its mother, who is then ready to mate and produce her next offspring. As the cub becomes more adventurous, it enjoys playing on fallen logs and climbing trees. The roly-poly body is perfect for rolling or somersaulting down a slope. Come winter, young pandas enjoy tumbling in the snow or tobogganing down a snow-covered slope.

Playing in the wintertime, an immature panda slides on its back down a snow-covered slope.

Much has been learned since the first panda was born in captivity at Beijing Zoo in 1963. During the first decade after the Captive Breeding Centre at Hetauping in Wolong was opened in 1983, it produced just one baby panda, in 1986, who died three years later. As the natural pairing of pandas was encouraged in preference to artificial insemination, the proportion of live births increased. In addition, the cubs now have a better chance of survival as the techniques for reducing neonatal mortality have improved. Indeed, in recent years eleven babies survived out of sixteen produced from eleven litters. The biologists at Hetauping have discovered that captive nursing mothers are very partial to golden-leafed bamboo. Now this species of bamboo is grown near the breeding center specifically to feed nursing mothers.

Captive pandas can be induced to breed as young as three-and-a-half years of age—two years earlier on average than wild pandas. The optimum breeding age for both male and female captives, however, is seven to sixteen years. Offspring reared by first-time mothers have a poor survival rate. But by weaning captive four-to-six-month-old infants from their mothers, the females are induced to come into estrus annually instead of biennially, which greatly increases the breeding potential of captive animals. Natural breeding and mother-reared captives seem to have a better chance of survival than cubs produced as a result of artificial insemination and hand-rearing.

A young panda watches the world from its vantage point in a tree high above the forest floor.

Scientists at the Wolong Breeding Centre have produced a detailed account of the development of a hand-reared infant that was abandoned by a mother who produced twins. They found the newborn crawled in the incubator for the first three days, when its forelimbs could support its body. As the infant grew heavier, it became more immobile; by twenty days, the forelimbs were no longer able to support the body. Not until the cub was two-and-a-half

A fallen tree trunk makes an exciting place for a one-year-old panda to play.

months was it able to crawl again using its forelimbs. When it was three months old, it could hold bamboo sticks in its forepaws, and, at four months, it could crawl easily.

Maternal neonatal care is very difficult to replicate. Young hand-reared infants are particularly vulnerable to picking up infections; many die from pneumonia. Before 1991, all attempts at rearing an infant panda on artificial formulas had failed. Powdered milk and fresh milk, as well as natural milk from goats, cows, dogs, and cats have all been fed to infant pandas in the past. Providing the correct temperature and humidity at each stage of the infant's development is essential. Initially, the incubator is maintained at 91° to 95°F (33° to 35°C) and at 65 to 67 percent humidity, but as the infant's coat begins to develop, both are reduced.

Lying amongst ferns, a young panda clutches a bamboo cane in each hand.

In addition to the existing breeding enclosures at Hetauping, a large breeding complex was completed in 1996 to accommodate ten more young pandas. Each of the ten enclosures is equipped with video monitoring. The scientists at Hetauping aim to have forty captive pandas by the year 2000, without capturing any more wild pandas. Ultimately, the researchers hope to release some of the captive-bred pandas back into the wild, instead of simply increasing the ratio of captive to wild pandas.

A young panda climbs to a perch within a pine tree.

Red Pandas

The red or lesser panda, although known to the Western world for almost half a century before the giant panda, has never evoked the affection showered upon its larger black-and-white relative. In 1869—the very year Père David saw his first giant panda skin—the first live red panda arrived at London Zoo.

Zoologists continue to debate how the red panda—which looks more like a raccoon than a bear, but exhibits both bearlike and raccoonlike characteristics—should be classified. Some argue it should remain in its own family—the *Ailuridae*—while others believe it should be placed in the same family as the giant panda. It has a wider distribution than the giant panda, ranging from parts of the Himalayas in Nepal, Bhutan, and Tibet in the west, to parts of northern Burma and the Chinese provinces of Sichuan and Yunnan in the east. Two distinct subspecies are recognized: the slightly larger Styan's lesser panda *(Ailurus fulgens styani)* in the east, and *Ailurus fulgens fulgens* in the west.

Even though the tree species within the red panda's mixed forest habitat vary from Nepal to China, bamboo is always present within the understory. Like the giant panda, the red panda requires a ready supply of bamboo, although it is by no means totally dependent on it, and will supplement the bamboo diet with lichens and the leaves, fruits, and roots of various plants. In the spring, the red panda is especially partial to birds' eggs and young birds.

In China, red and giant pandas live harmoniously together—even when their territories overlap. Indeed, red pandas in China benefit by sharing giant panda reserves, where clear-cutting is prohibited. The more agile red panda, however, is also able to survive on steeper and higher slopes (up to 13,120 feet /4,000 meters).

Except when mating, this relatively shy animal leads a solitary life, spending much time during daylight sleeping high up in tree forks or in natural hideaways beneath rocks or fallen trees. Red pandas favor territories on south-facing slopes, where they can sunbathe in treetops. The warmth from the sun helps them conserve their energy and reduce their feeding time. Being crepuscular (active at dawn and dusk) as well as nocturnal, red pandas descend from trees to feed early and late in the day. They may also drink in a stream early in the morning. During the cold winter months, however, they invariably wait until the air temperature begins to warm up before they become active.

A red, or lesser, panda walks over snow-covered rocks in the Wolong Reserve.

The alternative Chinese name of fire fox seems particularly apt when the lesser panda's reddish back is glimpsed as it weaves its way through vegetation or up and over rocks. A more leisurely look—through binoculars or a long lens—as the panda freezes to stare at an intruder, reveals a large head with pointed ears edged in white fur, a foxy snout, and distinctive white face markings. The reddish-brown bushy tail—marked with nine darker rings—and the dark brown belly and legs are most apparent as a red panda moves over snow or climbs a tree. Almost as long as its body, the red panda's tail serves both as a pillow and, in cold weather, as a most effective blanket by preventing heat loss when wrapped around the sleeping animal.

The red panda has an enlarged wrist bone that forms a sixth digit, or "thumb," on each front paw. Although this thumb is not as well developed as the giant panda's, the red panda uses the digit to grasp and pull down bamboo—and other plant stems—when feeding. Instead of sitting or lying down to feed, red pandas stand on the ground so they can reach the lower bamboo leaves and will climb onto rocks or fallen tree trunks to reach higher leaves.

With an essentially herbivorous diet and a digestive system typical of a carnivore, the red panda digests only about 25 percent of the dry matter that it eats, so it has to consume 30 percent of its body weight daily. This means it has to be active for about eight hours in every twenty-four-hour period.

Red pandas mate from January to March, when there is often snow on the ground. Because implantation of the embryo in the uterus is delayed, the gestation period varies from 112 to 158 days. A hollow tree or a rock cave is used as a breeding den, which a female lines with leaves and branches. When the cubs are born in June or July, they are blind and helpless, weighing only 4 to 5 ounces (110 to 130 grams). The father takes no part in raising the family. When born, the cubs are covered with buff-colored fur and are better developed (and marginally heavier) than giant panda newborns. For three weeks after she gives birth, the mother leaves her den for brief intervals to drink, to forage for food, and to defecate. After seventeen or eighteen days, the cubs' eyes open, and, after only seventy days, adult coloration develops fully.

For three to four months the cubs feed solely on their mother's milk. By September, they begin to sample bamboo, and by the time winter sets in they are completely weaned. If a den is discovered by humans, the mother detects the scent and may move her cubs. Should the cubs be encountered a second time, she may react by eating her offspring.

A constant stream of vociferous zoo visitors may jeopardize breeding success. Indeed, success rates in

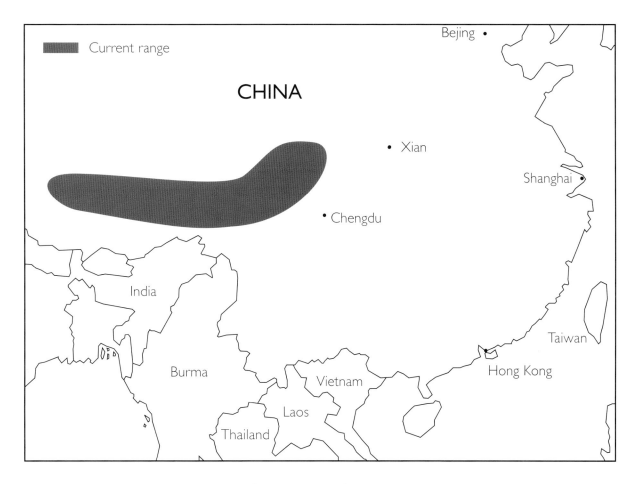

Current range of the red panda

captivity are still very low, despite the fact that red pandas become sexually mature at eighteen months and produce larger litters (two to four cubs) at more frequent intervals than the giant panda.

Arrow bamboo, the favorite food of the red panda, is also eaten by the giant panda.

Red pandas are highly territorial. From a study of nine individuals in Nepal, it is clear both males and females stake out their patch by marking scent posts around the periphery of their territories with their anal glands. In addition, the animals brush the ground with a palm scent produced from pores on the soles of their hairy feet. Red pandas use small protuberances beneath the tip of their tongue to detect scented calling cards left on rocks, trees, or the ground. When a male encounters another male during the breeding season and neither gives way, they will fight either by standing up on their hind legs and boxing with claws extended on their forepaws, or by rolling over, locked in combat, on the ground. During these confrontations, fur may fly as the animals fight, hissing and spitting at each other, reminiscent of dueling cats.

Before red pandas were protected, they were hunted in Nepal for their fur, which was made into caps. In China the tails were once prized as dusters. Greater success rates with captive breeding programs are required before any animals can be introduced into their natural home to boost the gene pool among wild populations. But, as with the giant panda, the native habitat of the endearing fire fox also must be conserved to protect the endangered animal.

After a fight, a red panda retreats up a tree, bearing blood-stained ears.
Red pandas typically spend most of the day up trees.

Conservation

By the mid-1990s, the population of giant pandas in the wild had dropped to about just 1,000 individuals—maybe half of the population that existed in Père David's day. At one time, pandas ranged over much of southeastern China. Today, they are confined to six isolated mountain ranges—a mere fraction of their historical range. The panda's survival is threatened not only by habitat loss, but also by accidental capture in snares set for musk deer, sought for their lucrative musk glands. Although the panda is protected, illegal transactions can bring in as much as $200,000 in U.S. currency for a single pelt in Japan, so a few poachers are willing to risk life imprisonment or even the death sentence.

In 1989, WWF and the Chinese Ministry of Forestry published a conservation management plan for the giant panda. The document outlined the problems facing pandas and proposed various steps to conserve the natural stock. These steps include setting up fourteen new nature reserves and training guards to patrol them, planting bamboo corridors to link the existing thirteen fragmented panda reserves, releasing captive offspring into the wild, and relocating peasant farmers.

If bamboo corridors are created by staggering the time of planting bamboo native to each area, the benefit to the pandas would be twofold: It would ensure a ready supply of food, and it would enable pandas (and other animals) to move freely between reserves to breed with different stock, thus preventing the dangers of genetic isolation and inbreeding. Research by scientists at San Diego Zoo into the way their captive pandas react to scent markings may prove invaluable for persuading wild pandas to walk through the green corridors. If it is found that pandas can be attracted by scent lures, reluctant individuals could be enticed to move to a new location.

By 1992, the main proposals of the conservation management plan had been incorporated and approved at an estimated cost of $63.5 million in U.S. currency, spread over a ten-year period. Since 1980, WWF has made significant and substantial contributions toward panda conservation, including constructing and equipping the breeding center at Wolong and funding field research by Pan Wenshi in the Qinling Mountains, home to about 200 pandas. While part of the plan will be financed from within China, substantial contributions will have

Propped up against a tree, a panda feeds in winter.

This page and facing page: A giant panda climbs a tree by hugging the trunk with its forearms and using its claws to grip the bark. It descends rapidly—like a firefighter sliding down a pole.

to come from overseas. Pandas sent on international long-term loans to zoos (such as the twelve-year loan to San Diego Zoo) could provide a lucrative source of funds. For the welfare of pandas, however, only captive-bred individuals should be exported in the future. Since Su Lin's capture in 1936, about 200 pandas have been removed from the wild, either shot for museum pelts or taken alive for zoos (both overseas and in China), and bamboo die-offs in the 1970s and 1980s may have resulted in the death of another 250 pandas. Then, summer 1997 brought news that thirty giant pandas had been discovered in a new area in northwestern Gansu Province. Whether good or bad, as news of pandas hits the headlines, it generates worldwide concern for their survival and inspires individual contributions toward their conservation via bodies such as WWF.

Although several other species of animals—including the Arabian oryx—have seen a wild population plummet below the current giant panda population, they are no longer endangered because they breed easily in captivity. Even with improved habitat protection, unless captive breeding becomes more successful, the panda has a bleak outlook for survival. With higher success rates, the release of captive-born pandas into the wild becomes a more feasible, albeit lengthy, process. Zhang Hemin, director of the Wolong Breeding Centre, tells how two pandas escaped into the wild—one in 1987, the other in 1991. They were recaptured after a few months, having lost almost a quarter of their weight, unable to fend for themselves in the wild, partly because their diet had been modified to include only a fraction of the bamboo eaten by wild pandas.

Releases of captive pandas will have to be carefully monitored. The Wolong Breeding Centre proposes to build a 2.3-square-mile (6-sq-km) enclosure in the forest near the center, into which a panda fitted with a radio collar will be released. Initially, some supplementary food will be provided, until the panda is able to forage for itself. If the panda has managed to maintain its weight after two years, it will be fitted with a new radio collar before being released at a higher elevation. Even without release programs, the training of guards to patrol the reserves must be given a high priority to ensure that wild pandas are protected.

It is fortunate that the giant panda lives in such a species-rich area, because investment and energies devoted to conserving its habitat will protect not only this charismatic species, but also a host of other animals and plants. Provided the wild panda population does not suffer any further setbacks and the necessary funding is realized, conservation efforts may yet save the giant panda. Indeed, the newborn baby that Pan Wenshi and Lu Zhi studied in the Qinling Mountains was christened Xi Wang—meaning "hope." Naturalists and conservationists the world over echo the sentiments of these Chinese biologists, but familiarity and affection alone will not be enough to save the bumbling, bamboo-eating panda from extinction.

The view across the Pitiao River Valley in winter shows farm houses and agricultural land encroaching on the lower slopes and forests that are home to the pandas.

A giant panda stands between two tree trunks.

Panda Facts

Giant panda

Chinese name: *da xiong mao* (large bear-cat)

Scientific name: *Ailuropoda melanoleuca*

Adult height: 5–6 feet (150–180 cm) when standing

Adult weight: 165–242 pounds (75–110 kg)

Longevity: unknown in the wild; up to 30 years in captivity

Newborn: 2.6–5.3 ounces (75–150 g); 0.11 percent of the mother's body weight

Gestation: 97–163 days (including delayed implantation of 1–3.5 months)

Breeding: sexually mature at 5.5–6.5 years

Litter size: 1, 2, or, rarely, 3 cubs. The mother is usually only able to care for the strongest one, which is often the firstborn; any others are left to die.

Red or lesser panda

Local names: Chinese: *xiao xiong mao* (small bear-cat) and *hon-ho* (fire fox)

Nepalese: *nigalya ponya* (bamboo eater)

Scientific name: *Ailurus fulgens styani* (Styan's lesser panda) and *Ailurus fulgens fulgens*

Adult head and body length: 20–25 inches (50–62.5 cm)

Adult tail length : 11–19 inches (28–48 cm)

Adult weight: 8.1–13.6 pounds (3.7–6.2 kg)

Longevity: up to 14 years

Newborn: 4–5 ounces (110–130 g)

Gestation: 112–158 days (including delayed implantation)

Breeding: sexually mature at 18–20 months

Litter size: 1–4 (usually 2) cubs

Index

Recommended Reading

Anyone interested in pandas should read two books by George B. Schaller, a zoologist who carried out pioneering research work on giant pandas in Wolong during the early 1980s. The *Giant Pandas of Wolong* (University of Chicago Press, 1985) is a most informative scientific account of the work by his research team. *The Last Panda* (University of Chicago Press, 1993) reviews the status of the panda at that time and comments on the missed opportunities. Keith and Elizabeth Laidler are a husband and wife biologist/filmmaker team who have spent much time filming in China, and their book *Pandas, Giants of the Bamboo Forest* (BBC Books, 1992) is a highly readable account of the panda's habitat and way of life. Ruth Harkness gives her own account of bringing the first live panda out of China in *The Lady and the Panda* (Nicholson and Watson, 1938). An introduction to the natural history, biology, and plight of the giant panda can be found in Barbara Radcliffe Rogers's book *Giant Pandas* (Michael Friedman Publishing Group, 1994).

Biographical Note

Author and photographer Heather Angel.
Photo © by Derek Tamea.

Heather Angel with young panda.
Photo © by John Giustina.

Heather Angel trained as a zoologist and worked as a marine biologist before becoming a professional wildlife photographer. She has visited China twelve times, including four visits specifically to photograph pandas. While she was president of the Royal Photographic Society, she led a small British photographic delegation to China in 1985, when an exhibition of her wildlife photographs was staged in Beijing. In 1994, she was appointed a special professor at Nottingham University, where she teaches part of the photography module. In 1998, she was elected as the Louis Schmidt Laureate by the Biological Photographic Association. Professor Angel lives in England.